The Nature Kid's Guide to
HORSES

DAVID ANDERSON

LP Media Inc. Publishing
Text copyright © 2026 by LP Media Inc.

For information address LP Media Inc. Publishing,
30012 Variolite St NW, Princeton MN 55371
www.lpmedia.org

Publication Data

Horses
The Nature Kid's Guide to Horses — First edition.

Summary: "Learn all about Horses, the Nature Kid Way"
— Provided by publisher.

ISBN: 979-8-89818-194-9

[1. Horses – Non-Fiction] I. Title.

Title: The Nature Kid's Guide to Horses

CONTENTS

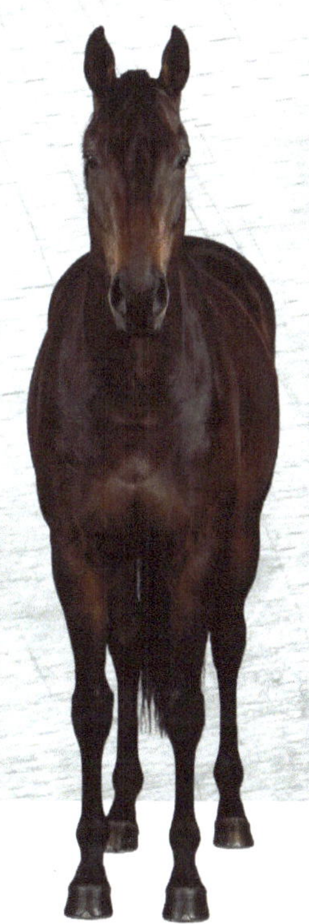

HORSES AMAZE

Horses sleep standing up! Special leg joints lock in place so they don't fall over.

Clip-clop! A horse trots across a sunny green meadow.

Horses are one of the most amazing animals on Earth. For over 5,000 years, they have worked beside us, carried us into battle, and raced us across open plains. No other animal has shaped human history quite like the horse.

Today, horses still capture our hearts. Some thunder around racetracks. Others work cattle on dusty ranches or pull giant wagons in parades. Many are simply best friends to the people who ride them.

From the tiniest Falabella no bigger than a dog to the mighty Clydesdale that shakes the ground with every step, get ready to meet some incredible **breeds**.

HOOVES AND HEARTS

A horse's teeth take up more space in its head than its brain does!

Thump-thump! A horse's big heart beats strong and steady.

A horse's body is built for running. Strong muscles fill its legs and back. Long legs help it take big steps and move fast.

Hooves are like tough shoes. They protect a horse's feet on hard ground. Each **hoof** is made of the same stuff as your fingernails! A **farrier** must trim them every six to eight weeks.

A horse has a very big heart. It can weigh up to 10 pounds. That powerful heart pumps blood to all those big muscles, giving a horse its amazing strength.

SENSING STALLIONS

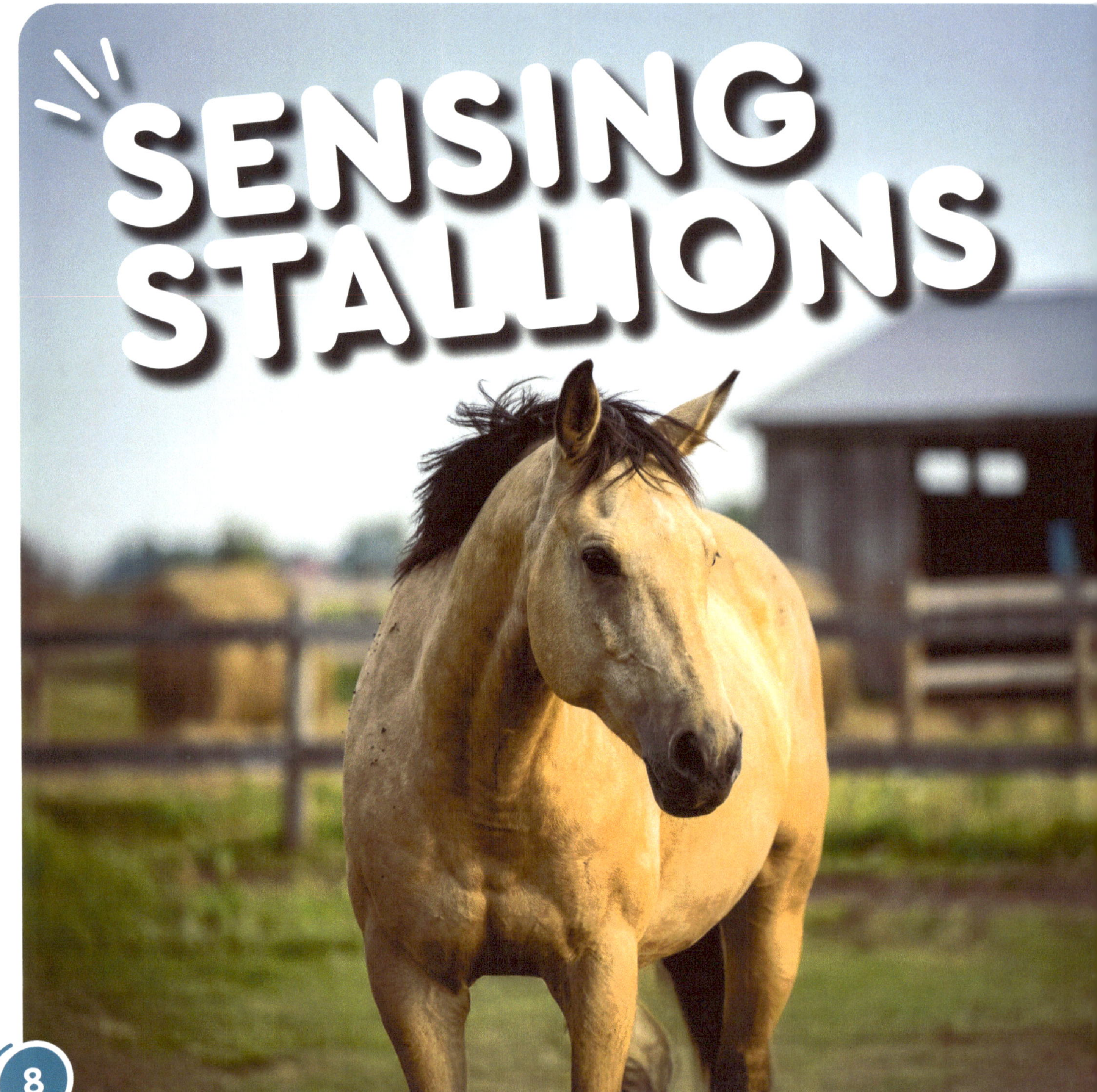

Whoosh! A horse flicks its ears toward a far-off sound.

Horses have amazing senses. Their big eyes sit on the sides of their head, letting them see almost all the way around without turning.

Each ear can turn on its own. A horse can point one ear forward and one back at the same time, picking up sounds from every direction.

Horses also have a great sense of smell. They can sniff the air and tell if a friend is near, or find water from far away.

A horse can see two different things at once, one with each eye!

DESERT BEAUTIES

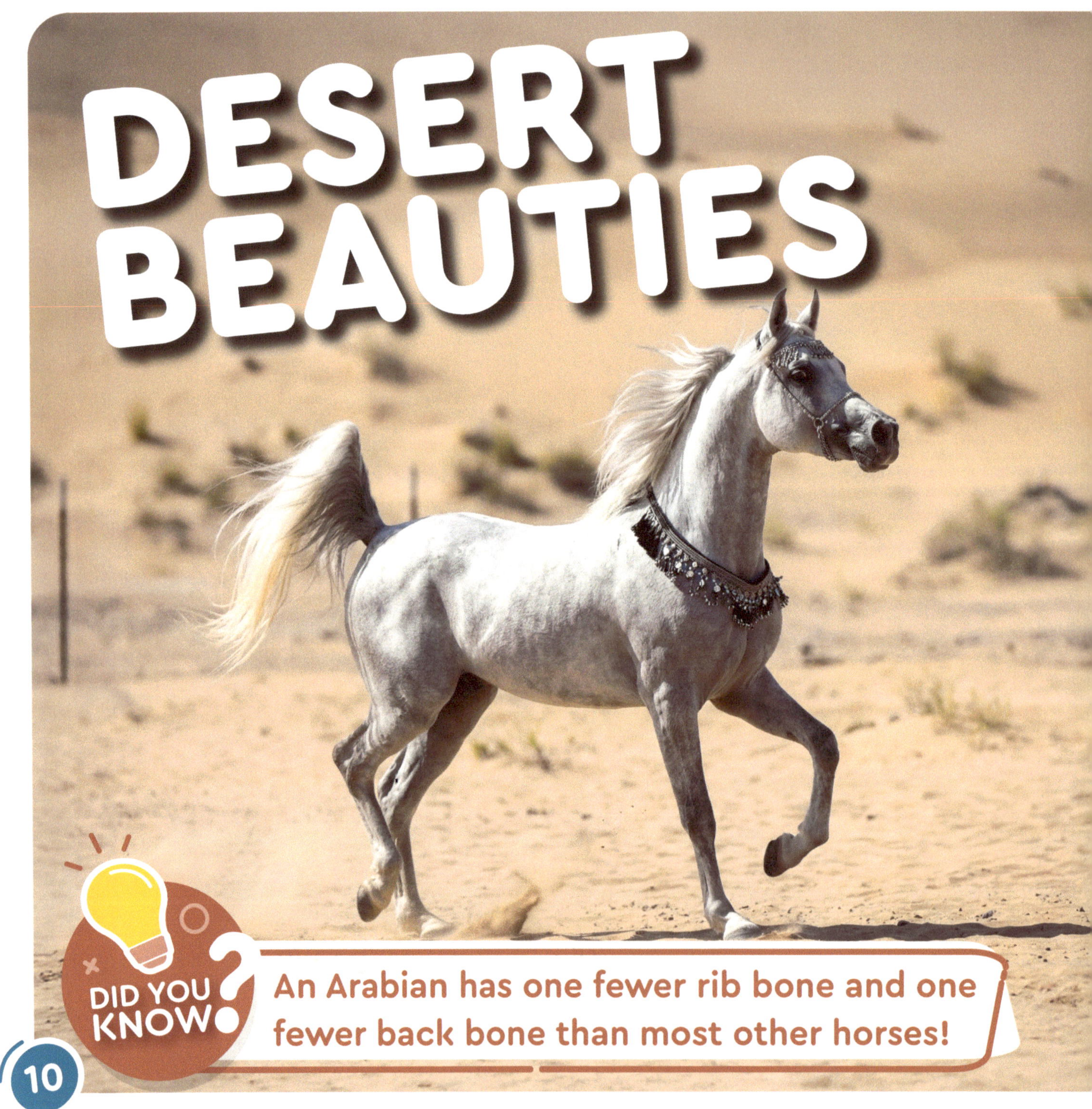

10

Swish! An Arabian prances through warm desert sand.

Arabian horses come from the hot deserts of the Middle East. They are one of the oldest horse breeds. People have loved them for over 4,500 years.

These horses have wide noses. Big nostrils help them breathe the dry, dusty air. Their bodies stay cool even in strong heat.

Arabians have a face that curves inward. Their tails arch up high when they run. Watching them move, they look like they are dancing on the sand.

RACING ROYALTY

Zoom! A Thoroughbred flies past the finish line first.

Thoroughbreds are built to race. They have long legs and lean bodies. Every part of them is made for speed.

These horses got their start in England about 300 years ago. Breeders mixed fast horses to make even faster ones. Today, Thoroughbreds race on tracks all over the world.

A Thoroughbred can run very fast. It can reach speeds near 45 miles per hour. That is faster than a car driving on a city street!

All Thoroughbreds alive today can trace their family back to just three horses from the 1700s!

QUARTER HORSES

Whomp! A Quarter Horse darts after a running calf.

Quarter Horses are the most popular breed in America, with millions living across the country. They are calm, smart, and learn quickly, which is why so many people love them.

These horses are built for power. Thick muscles in their back legs help them stop and turn in a flash. Cowboys use them for working cattle on ranches.

Quarter Horses are also the fastest breed over short distances. They can burst to top speed in just a few steps.

A Quarter Horse can reach 55 miles per hour in a short sprint.

SPOTTED STALLIONS

An Appaloosa's spotted coat pattern can change as the horse grows older!

Neigh! A spotted Appaloosa runs across the grassy hills.

Appaloosas are easy to spot. They have bold patterns of dots and patches on their coats. No two Appaloosas look exactly the same.

The Nez Perce people of Idaho raised these horses long ago. They picked the strongest and most beautiful ones to breed. This made the Appaloosa smart, tough, and loyal.

Appaloosas also have striped hooves. Their skin has spots under the fur too. Even their eyes sometimes have white rings around them. They are spotted inside and out!

PAINTED PONIES

Whinny! A bright Paint Horse gallops through a wide field.

Paint Horses wear big patches of white and color. Each horse has its own special look. Some have more white. Others have more brown or black.

No two Paint Horses look the same. Some have white splashed across their back. Others have white on their belly or face. It is like every one was painted by a different artist!

Paint Horses are strong and friendly. They do well on ranches and in shows. Kids love them because each one looks like a living painting.

SHETLAND POWER

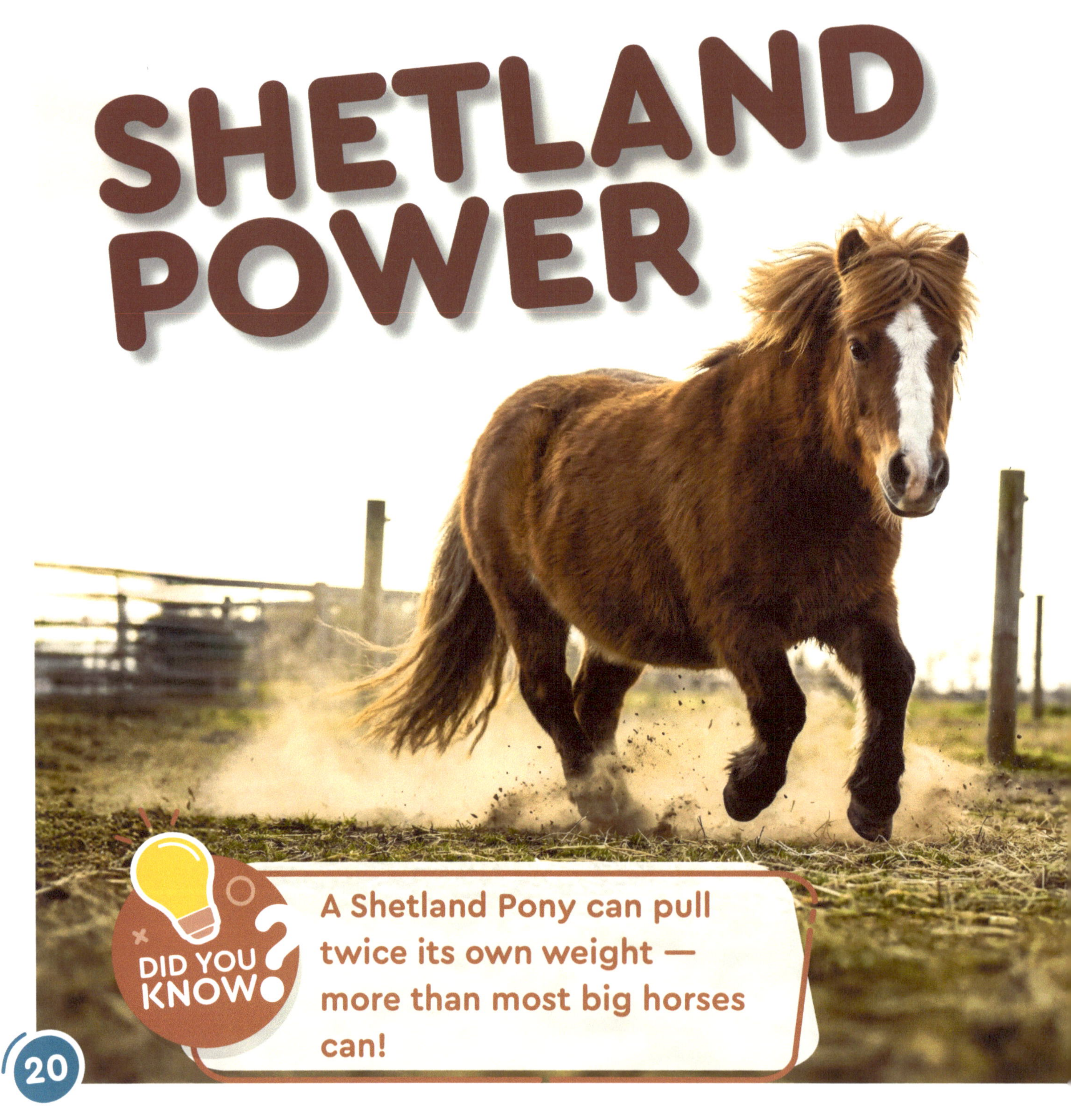

A Shetland Pony can pull twice its own weight — more than most big horses can!

Stomp! A tiny Shetland Pony kicks up dust with its small hooves.

Shetland Ponies come from cold, windy islands near Scotland. They are one of the smallest horse breeds, standing only about 3 feet tall. But do not let their size fool you!

These ponies are very strong. Long ago, they pulled heavy carts of coal in dark mines. Their thick, shaggy coats keep them warm in icy wind and rain.

Shetland Ponies are great for young riders. They are gentle and fun to be around. Many kids learn to ride on these little ponies first.

BLACK MAJESTY
22

Swoosh! A Friesian's long black mane waves in the breeze.

Friesians are big, shiny black horses. They come from a part of the Netherlands called Friesland.

These horses have long, flowing manes and tails. Their hair can reach nearly to the ground! They look like horses from a fairy tale.

Friesians move with high, proud steps. They are often seen in parades and movies. Their beauty and grace make them real stars wherever they go.

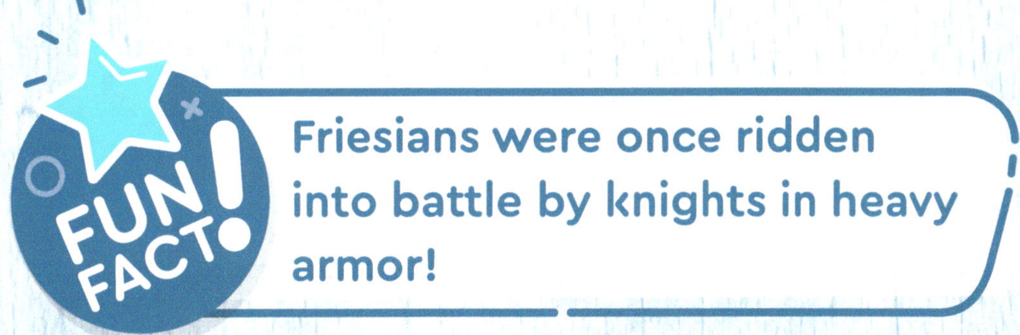

Friesians were once ridden into battle by knights in heavy armor!

GIANTS MARCH

Boom! A giant Clydesdale shakes the ground with each step.

Clydesdales are one of the biggest horse breeds. They can stand over six feet tall at the shoulder. That is taller than most grown-ups!

These horses come from Scotland. Farmers once used them to pull heavy plows through thick soil. Today, they are famous for pulling big wagons in parades and shows.

Clydesdales have long, silky hair on their lower legs. This hair is called **feathering**. Their big hooves are the size of dinner plates, and each one weighs about five pounds.

MIGHTY BELGIANS

Thud! A Belgian Draft pulls a heavy log with ease.

Belgian Draft horses are gentle giants. They have wide chests and thick necks. Their strong bodies are built for pulling heavy loads.

These big horses come from Belgium in Europe. Farmers used them for the hardest work on the farm. A team of two Belgians was stronger than any tractor.

Most Belgians have sandy brown coats and light manes. Even though they are huge, they are calm and easy to handle.

Two Belgian horses once pulled over 17,000 pounds — that's heavier than three cars!

CURVED-EAR CHAMPS

Click-click! A Marwari turns its curved ears toward you.

Marwari horses come from India. They are easy to know because of their special ears. The tips curve inward so much that they can touch each other!

Long ago, warriors rode the brave Marwaris into battle. Legends say they wouldn't run away from danger, even when hurt.

Marwaris can walk in a smooth, gliding way. This makes the ride feel gentle and easy. In India, they still perform at weddings and festivals today.

Marwari horses are so rare that India once banned sending them to other countries!

GOLDEN STALLIONS

Flash! An Akhal-Teke gleams like gold in the bright sun.

Akhal-Tekes are sometimes called golden horses. Their coat has a special shine that no other breed has. It can look like metal glowing in the sunlight.

These horses come from the hot deserts of Turkmenistan. The harsh climate made them tough and fast. They can run long distances without much water.

Akhal-Tekes are tall and slim with thin skin and sleek bodies. Many people call them the most beautiful horses on Earth.

There are only about 6,000 Akhal-Teke horses left in the whole world!

TINY FOALS

Squeak! A tiny Falabella foal is no bigger than a dog.

Falabellas are the smallest horses in the world. A full-grown one stands only about 30 inches tall. That is shorter than a big dog!

These tiny horses come from Argentina. The Falabella family chose only the smallest horses to have babies. Over many years, each new **foal** was smaller than the last.

Falabellas are too small to ride. But people keep them as pets instead. They are sweet and playful, just like a puppy with hooves.

A newborn Falabella foal weighs only about 12 pounds!

WILD WARRIORS

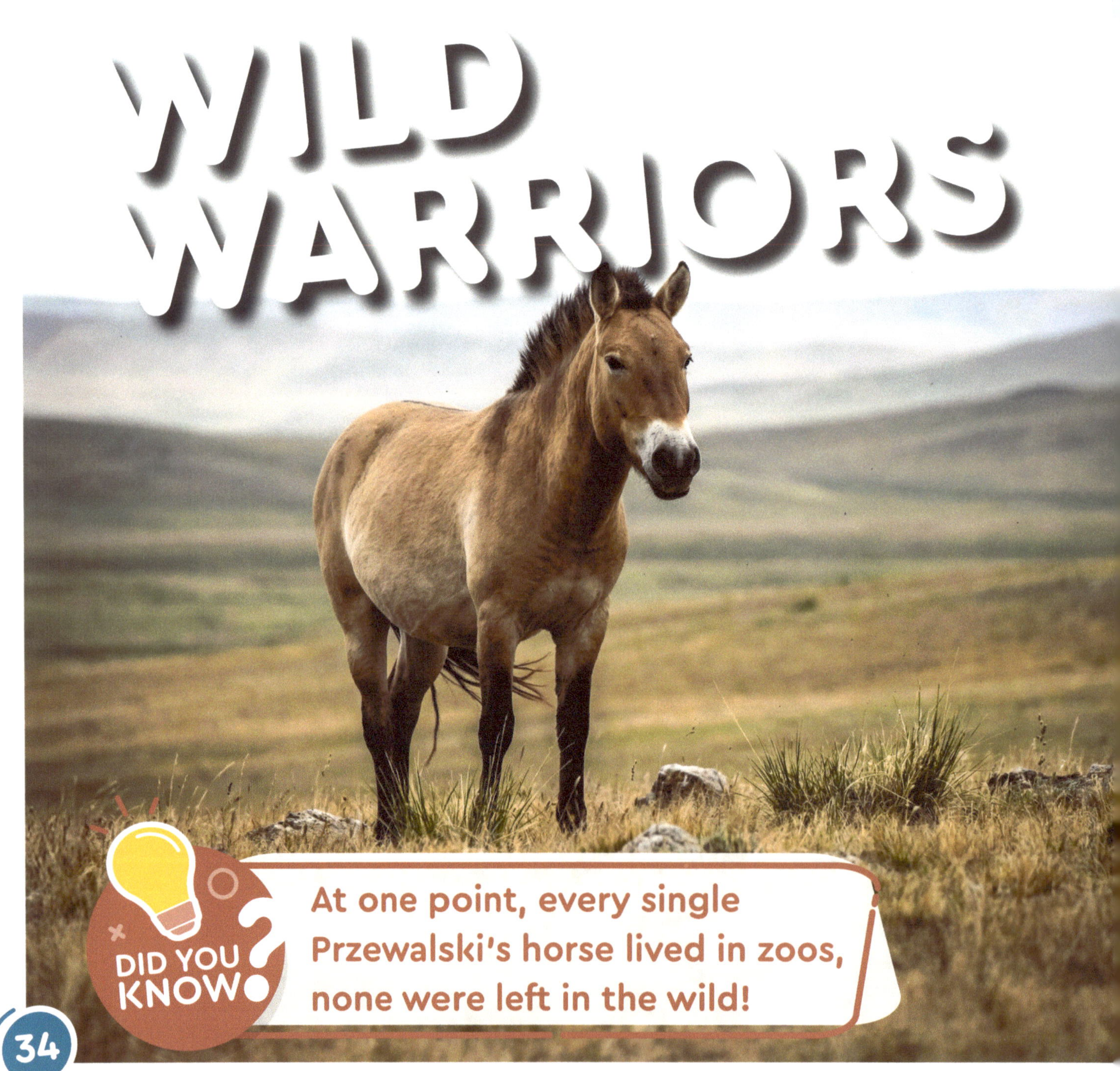

Snort! A wild Przewalski's horse watches from the hilltop.

Przewalski's horse is the last truly wild horse breed. It has never been tamed by people. These tough horses live on the dry grasslands of Mongolia.

They have short, stiff manes that stand straight up like a brush. Their bodies are thick and strong. A dark stripe runs down their back from head to tail.

Przewalski's horses almost died out long ago. By 1969, only 12 were left. People worked hard to save them. Now small herds run free in the wild once again.

MUSTANGS RUN

Thunder! A herd of wild mustangs races across the plains.

Mustangs are free horses that roam the American West. They live in herds across deserts, mountains, and wide open plains. No one owns them.

Long ago, Spanish explorers brought horses to America. Some of those horses escaped and became wild. Over hundreds of years, their families grew into big herds.

A lead mare guides each herd to food and water. A strong stallion keeps the group safe from danger. Mustangs are smart, tough, and true survivors of the wild.

HORSE LOVE

FUN
FACT!

A horse can eat for up to
17 hours each day if it has
enough grass!

Munch! A happy horse gets a sugar cube from its rider.

Taking care of a horse is a big job, but horse lovers would not trade it for anything. Every morning starts with feeding, filling water buckets, and saying hello to a friend who is always happy to see you.

The best part is **grooming**. Brushing the coat until it shines, combing out the mane and tail, and picking dirt from the hooves. Horses love the attention, and it is how you build a bond nothing can break.

Riding is the biggest thrill of all. It takes practice, but once you and your horse move together, there is no better feeling in the world.

GLOSSARY

breed
A specific type of horse with shared features

farrier
A person who trims and cares for a horse's hooves

feathering
The long, silky hair that grows on the lower legs of some horse breeds.

foal
A baby horse

hoof
The hard covering on a horse's foot

grooming
Brushing, combing, and cleaning a horse to keep it healthy and happy.